an open passage to

lizz matthews

© Lizz Matthews 2018
ISBN: 9781791748425

for my mother, audrey elizabeth
and my aunt, teri nicole.
thank you for looking out for me when no one
else did. i love you endlessly.

find your way.

i love my father
i need my father
my father knows me
my father is a hero
i look up to him

he always said
"i love you,"

you
you
you
you

hello

an open passage to truant fathers

once you have left, don't come back
and tell me you never left me

as if i am not lying in you and mom's bed every night
fighting the urge to smash a glass statuette that
reads "dad"
that i bought you for christmas when i was young
and staring at the picture of myself hidden by your
pill bottles
do not wake me at five in the afternoon
two weeks after leaving
saying you want me to live with you

and to a father's truant father,
i say that you must speak with him

tell him he was wrong,
that you were wrong
that you are sorry for what you had done
and that he doesn't know how good he has it
how good he had it
and i pray like the last time i prayed as a child
for daddy not to stay gone too long
to any god, to anyone

i just hope that the only man i see at home anymore
doesn't leave his loved ones, too

and to my mother's truant father
i ask, what can you do?

what can you do to redeem yourself
by showing a beautiful woman she matters
when the person she loves the most
treats her like she doesn't
what did you do those many times that you left them
and do you regret it now?

to all the truant fathers

who have strayed from the bed
their daughter is lying on,
their daughter is crying on,
their daughter is dying on:

do you regret it now?

11/18/2017

she is shut away
she disappeared
no physicality, she is not

here

i don't want talking anymore,
i want silence

silence

like sitting in the basement with headphones on,
holding the end of the cord in your sweaty palms
your knuckles pressed against your chest
and you wonder what the earliest memory you have
saved in your mind is
what the happiest memory you can recall is
you try to remember every single birthday party you
had and every birthday party you weren't invited to
you remembered his eyes
his face
his smile, his laugh
you remembered your parents when they were happy
when they seemed happy
when they were the first wax figurines you'd seen
and the coldest sea
he used to wear a gold chain and she would faint in
the hallways
he would drag the burning couch and she'd carry you
from the flames
he would grab her by the waist and she would smile
while they kissed
and you were disgusted because you knew that was real
love
they said it was real love
you wanted real love
so you hurt the one person you loved the most to

achieve it
you lied to the person you loved the most to achieve
it
because that's all you were ever taught to do in this
world
and look how far that's gotten you
look how far that's gotten them

here you are rotting by a vent listening to the clock
on the wall and all you can think of is tryptophan
and ceiling fans
the closet before you
the closet your friend had you sleep in
the bed that feels better than your own because it is
associated with lone and not with home
you think from an aerial view of the times you laid
on cold, concrete floors because you wanted to feel
something
you think from an addicted view of the times you
slit, slashed, and scratched because you wanted to
feel something
you think of the times they had to light that
cigarette to reach solid ground and you just wanted
them to feel something
you wanted to be something
you wanted to be anything
you wish you could take all the pain away
you wish you could take it all back

i wish i could be something to you
i wish i could be anything to you

i wish i could be a better sister
or even just a sister

i wish i could be angel again
we were all happier then
we all seemed happier then

i wish i could get past the hospital parking lot
i wish i could put you back in your respective spot

i wish i could do anything to show you that what you
see is not a reality

that we are living in a dream
and there's no way for me to save myself
and there's no way for me to save you from pain

i wish i could
i wish we could remember
i wish i could feel the silence and the cord in my
hand
feel something, anything
that feels like family
that feels like home, again

i feel as though my childhood is best represented
in a rainbow and black mandala
harsh lines that the ink runs over
and mistakes in the patterns
but it's trying
and there's sweet candy in the flowers
but it all comes back to thick borders
and black paisleys
blocking arches and lines of color
there's scales and twists and the paper is rough
with torn edges, it is split in four sections
divided, with folds
and the red is the only color that bleeds through
other than black
when you look on the other side
my life is represented in this mandala
that i created from nothing
and turned into something
that i wouldn't necessarily call beautiful
but it tried
and i tried.

narcissus

rose gold and navy
an extra "u" in things
i could never be a decision maker

don't touch any buttons
when you see my name
you are a personality faker

and when you come around to speak to me
don't begin saying you were my maker
a manufacturer, you were
but instead of my life, you made falsehood
an extra "you" to your own
but instead of your wife, you loved yourself
narcissus, i see through your reflection in the water
narcissus, i see right through you.

i sleep with my eyes on the gun cabinet and wonder
what the code to unlock it may be
and while i attempt to dream of men i'll never meet
all i can think of is the man who left me
who left us
the man who told them i'd never unlock it
i'd never be able to unlock it
but how many combinations could be in that small mind
of yours?

baby

you are so pretty

pretty for the eyes we see but don't sting
red lips under your nose and red bags above your
cheeks

you are so pretty

every time you cry for help, you always cry for help
to see yourself, why can't you see yourself?

you are so pretty

that face could make a widow blush but your brain is
mush
you are so pretty

the prettiest girl in the loony bin
and you'll be even prettier when
you feel those pills kick in

tiny poem; a final goodbye for austin

5/6/2017

i saw a bottle of nail polish had fallen over just as
i did.
i found myself comparing our relationship to the
fluid that leaked from the spout when it fell
it was sad. and potent. and beautiful.
drying up just as soon as it emerged
it was my favorite. and it made me happy. and it made
me confident.
but when you ignore nail polish, it chips.
you might even pick at it when you get nervous.
even though it was expensive. and took time. and took
work.
even if you want it, you think you can just apply
more later.
but what happens when you run out?
what happens when the bottle falls?
what happens when all the polish has gone to waste?
the brush still works but you have no more product.
one side of the equation falls and the whole thing is
done.
it was difficult to apply. i have shaky hands. you
have shaky hands too.
i had peeled off the label, so the color confused me.
our eyes are glazed blue but all i see is red.
red is the color of affection, and care, and anger,
and pain.
it is the color of blood whether it is sacrificed or
lost.
the color of the bracelet for me and blue for you.
but you never got that, did you?
because you ignored it. you ignored me. and we
chipped away.

saxapahaw-bethlehem

my hair is the colour of caramel
and it feels like it when it's greasy
when i haven't showered in a week
when insomnia says i can't sleep
i'm taking depression-fuelled naps till three
in the afternoon; and i'm tired, mama, i'm tired

green thoughts
are unsettling thoughts
that shake me, startle me
stop me in my tracks
like a hem
on the middle of the shin
and images of moving spheres under skin
make me bad
a vessel, a valley in my throat
in my medusa kissed tonsil
for the nausea and the vomiting
green thoughts and green cards
border walls and
green for go
run
or hide in churches
like a bookcase annex
because of little orange men
green thoughts are
lisa frank stickers at a crime scene
that confuse me
but what doesn't
and blood mistaken for
little red blooms
on my little
so little
feet
green thoughts are muted in
jade haze
and mutilate me with sage
smoke
me
like a cigar
and watching me spark
spark, away

december 28, 2017: the end of a diary entry

12/28/2017

the six stones in a row on my desktop
geometrical ornaments both iridescent and transparent
like moonstones
and two others
like chocolate rock candy and dalmation-dragon's
breath
in front of a shimmering grave reading "nevermore"
and pencils, in a cup

i see the light as it shines but only in reflections
and acknowledge it from shadows

i am eighteen today

but the frame in front of me says i'm nine
and the scissors beside me say i'm ten
or eleven

and the broken vase leaking toxic gas tells me i'm
old enough not to live anymore
along with the pains in my chest
agreeing with the weight on my foot

in my hand, an ache

noticing spelling errors and little mistakes
was my life a mistake that i can't escape
a big mistake

if you hadn't had me, would you be in this place

oh mama,
i don't just want to be okay
i want to be alive, but blind
to the villainy that binds me
and for the adhesive on my lungs to let go and let me
exhale

instead of feeling him hitting my head on that wall

oh for the love of everything on earth, could i be
happy?

could i stare at my bare body without wanting to see
more bone
could i stare at my bare body and not see someone's
property before me

for every person that i have ever loved could there
be one more happy molecule instead of happy pill

could you ease my pain
while letting me live

dear mama,
oh mama,
give me life again

the sunlight burns a hole in the table
and my eyes
oh, my eyes
how they ache from the pain of the saltwater

am i
an ocean, your body of water
your open shore, your red sea

why do i think of you
and your eyes
and the smell of strings on a bass
and your hands pulling my thighs

a part
of me says i deserved it
but that i didn't deserve you

but that on the other hand
the only man i should ever be able to score is a
rapist

yes, a rapist

and you laugh at the claim with your friends
and tell girls nothing ever happened with me

but were you high for half a year?
because i was the lowest of the low
the bottom of the barrel
the last straw
a barren ocean that left me
lonely enough to love a man
who hid my pain with more pain
like a razor blade to my skin

my land for five months,
disguised quicksand

and all i did
was allow you to look at me, lovingly
the water in a line on the horizon

but you polluted me
until i died, dust and dry

i remember my father's laugh
    i remember his deep set eyes
i remember the days he spent at home
    i remember the days ostracized

i remember the days he took me to camp
    i remember when he held our hearts in his hands

i remember the day he called me
i remember his every word
i remember the day he left me
i remember he said he left her

i remember taking family for granted
i remember thinking he'd only leave us if he died
i remember every time i tried to keep him happy
    i remember that i tried

what don't you understand about
        "i don't understand"

that this is the dread in every
        day that is dreadful

it is not because i don't like being
        here because i like being here

it is because every time i must
        find the slope of a graph, declining
        i see my own will to live
        as a twelve year old girl

i am transformed, flipped over the
        "why" axis into negative

        and i can feel the concrete wall
        on my back in "remediation math"
        while the girl beside me recommends
        what would become my favorite
        book but i don't have time to
        read it because i plan on dying
        soon

the flat line

and i'm so over life that it's dividing me
        piece by piece till
        i become lesser of a person

i remember that all the math
        i did in class was multiplying
        the cuts on my arm and subtracting
        meals

that the teachers screaming
        pierced my ears better than
        the ladies at claire's

but at least those holes healed

that my sixth grade algebra
        teacher grabbed my arm and
        twisted it backwards

i can't solve my own problems
        so how can you expect me
        to solve those

enjoy the silence
      no surprises
don't speak
      one of my turns

i want silence
and songs in my head
slow songs
sometimes sad songs
and for the pain not to hurt so bad

i want the pipes to touch my skin
and not the rope attached to them
although it seems like what i want
or that i want to be thin
and sometimes i may

i want my clavicles to protrude from my shoulders
and the blades to cut them
maybe my ribs like a xylophone
played with fleshy boulders
but not to be skinny

i want my breath to be cherished
and captured and treasured
like a goddess among earth
treating them how they worship me
and for there to be so much happiness
      it couldn't possibly be measured

but i also want silence

and happiness
no pain

i want silence

and contentment
a hushed brain

i want silence

not misery
not murder
no shame

in being silent
for a minute
like a game
for children
am i a child

i want silence

i want silence

and silence

my special cardigan is a woolen comfort envelope
an invisibility cloak
but only when i need it
a surefire symbol to the world indicating
introversion
and a pinch of awkward social interaction
my special cardigan radiates fuzz like a forcefield
saying, "don't touch me,
but i like being cuddled"
the worn buttons serve as proof of how special my
cardigan truly is
just like the holes in my shoes
as they are the two items in my closet that actually
fit me
perfectly
holding me
telling me that i, too, belong here
and that i, too, can be spoken for
my special cardigan is the perfect shade of pink
the only shade that i like
not too rough and not too thick,
fitting to my skin but not constricting it
my special cardigan is like an old friend
that i can't wait to see again.

i don't know why i like the feeling of drowning in my
own bathwater
or peeling the skin on my arm back like an orange
peel
but maybe it's because i feel empty
i'll do it because i feel empty

love is not pain
but the absence of it
and if we believe that it is
we may find ourselves seeking suffering

love is not suffering
or being suffocated
but being held afloat
supported, and gazed at, not looked down upon

love is not pain
forgiving someone when they abuse you
manipulation, exploitation
not seeing the problems

because we are told
"love is pain"
but i will not suffer
or be held under
when i can't swim
love is love
indescribable, enjoyable love
irreplaceable love

not anger, not pain, not suffering

love is the arms that hold you, not the ropes or zip-
ties

love is not pain

love is love

i smile
as he draws
and you play the guitar
and we dance
and we run
and when we regain composure
we find closure
in passive aggressive pestering
and sorrowful sighs, blue eyes
can you fix my hot chocolate for me?
can i fix you?

                    (a letter to) happy wednesday

happy wednesday, kill me
happy wednesday, why am i not?
happy wednesday, shouldn't i be?
after all, i've thrown life away

on faux leather and my laptop
and the fear i've broken what you told me not to

happy wednesday, can you sympathize with me
and the feeling of hands landing on my thighs again
exhilarating

happy wednesday, could you leave me in the alley
with a red and black blanket
kiss my nose and turn the flash off

for the sight of the federal building through my eyes
and the butterflies
are all i need to blind me

(a goodbye for b. a hello) for you.

        i hope you dream of me
        i hope you whisper my name
        i want you to love me the way i always wanted
        i want to save each other from pain

you want me to continue loving you
despite how much we've changed
you want me to promise we won't float away
but these days, promises aren't the same

        you want me to hold you while the lights move
        windows and cigarettes and trenchcoats and
blues

you want me to wait and to tolerate you
but i'm bored of the stories, and the vineyard, and
the same old news
i need you to respect me
if i end up hurting you
because no matter how far our ships float apart
there will always be room in my heart for

        you

i don't want to sit in a desk and see myself hanging
simply because i'm unhappy with you
and you're unhappy with my numbers
i can't wait until the clock reads forty-two
and i need to take a shower
i need him to hold me
and kiss me
and look me in the eyes and smile
i want to forget about everyone else
that's in love with him
i love him the most
"i love you the most"
he hates him the most
why are we so alone
with a yoga mat
and knee pads
praying angels
and folding chairs
a nightmare, a nightmare
i didn't want to tell you
but he had no disregard
he didn't hold back
but the other him
i couldn't hold back
i couldn't lean back
and i wanted him
so i let him
lean in

the smell of cigarettes coats my nostrils again
and my lungs
and i haven't felt you in hours
but i want to
your skin is like a rubber wrapping paper and your
hair, satin ribbon
let me unwravel you
you are the gift i have longed for my whole life
my love
and amongst all of the ashes, my pain is put out
all of my sorrow, and emptiness, and stress
she's smoking again, and drinking with friends
but you hold me, dizzy
austin, austin
a shivering, shaking masterpiece of man
call on me in my darkest hour
and calm me with your presence

  ritalin

i press on my head to ease the pain
and prevent the passing out of exhaustion
the shortness of breath
shorter than my hands and my feet
and my attention span

the tattoos on your shoulders and the scar on your
chest
help me remember
papa was a sign painter down in salinas
papa was a building sketcher down in guilford
with uncle memories of touring factories of
fluorescent felines
making you beaded candy canes
your seductress ceos
with their legs crossed, inverted
permanent dye jobs
getting laid off
in more than a few variations
"big bang baby, it's a crash, crash, crash"

take me (to the theatre)

leave me be
for the time being
in the puddles of ginger camouflage
as the ladybugs crawl over cuts on my neck
and i throw them with erasers
erase me
you raised me
and you told me not to love him
to look at him
i see the way you look at him
my little capulet

                    father's day: all of my feelings sink into
                                                          guilt

father's day
all of my feelings sink into guilt
like a rock sinking to the bottom of the ocean, my
anger
instead of remaining on the surface

you ask why i am the way i am towards you
as if the only feelings i have are anger
but my feelings go deeper than surface level

father's day
all of my feelings sink into guilt
instead of floating
dad, i don't know how to float
why didn't you teach me how to float?

you ask why i don't speak to you
and why when i do, i yell at you
you didn't teach me to float, dad, you taught me to
boil over
to hide my emotions in the mariana trench
to bottle them up like messages
sending out an sos

father's day
and i'm the one feeling guilty
dad,
why didn't you teach me not to care?

        scream, again: i tried to speak to him, but
                  find myself calling for mother

i don't want to live here anymore
nowhere i walk do i feel safe
no room i'm in do i not feel you
or hear the names my father called me
or see the bruises from the kids pushing me

i don't want to sleep here anymore
i don't know what you did to me while i slept
but i felt your hands the day after
and i feel them every time i wake up
in the room where you touched me

i don't want to hear him anymore, mother
his name, his voice on the porch
his bass buzzing, letting me know
i am still his instrument
the sound of his grip on my doorknob

mother, i don't want to be here anymore

repetition is the sincerest form of the
sincerest form of (abstract obstructions in
my seven o'clock bedroom)

all that's on my mind is
      sex and
      selective serotonin reuptake inhibitors

whether it's the good, the bad, or
      the chronic

my head in the clouds and my
      arm reading "platonic"

you don't want me to love him,
      but i do
      and i will

and it is unlike the unspeakable
      the liars and the fools

he loves me
      he does
      and he will

and he will respect me
      unlike you ever did

he will hold me
and calm me
and tell me i'm beautiful
you never did
      truly

so take the pill and feel it when
      you swallow
my wingspan is long enough, but
      i will never welcome you

like i did when we were younger

the liar and the fool

the liars and the fools
i am not one of you

but we are one
        and done
and we are done with you

        unspeakable

bacteria bodies and sad, droopy eyes
my tears erode dead cells like trails
torn, black sails
i'm lighting twinscence
and absinthe
they're rubbing off on you

i want him to kiss me
like a handwritten letter
wax seals
and satin quills
to call me
his opium poppy

and tear me apart
petal by petal
leaf by leaf
he loves me
he loves me not
big baby maturity
i know you tried
but you can't stop

take a moment, for me.
look through the tears that well up in your eyes
and tell me what you see

is it blurry? is it grey?
do you see your legs before you? don't blink
just listen to what i say

you are the dark
the spot in my eye, the migraine
the encapsulated, cocooned pharaoh, the burn mark

you are the shadow beneath my eye
the lines that leave me pacing
you are the hazy view of my thighs

of my hands
and my blue pants
and your fancy-dance
prancing about

you are the fence that tore my flesh while i walked
and the asphalt that burned my feet

the swimming pools that satiated my very being

and the bug buzzing in that ear, and the screaming,
and everything i couldn't hear

you are the and that connects me to the rest of me
the pieces that flinch and flutter around me
the paper in the silver room
the emptiness in the shade
and the riveting divots of my cerebellum that will
wrinkle in time.

the girl who stole orion's belt, a chevrolet seatbelt

the thumbtacks in the roof of dad's bmw are the
closest thing to stars i can get
holding my sky up like chicken little in the back
seat
fifteen year old thinking she's mature for her age
and i was
but she had no map of the road ahead
seven years old and looking at orion
to remind me of home
thinking seventeen years old would be
the best year of my life
a nice car
a happy family
a beautiful boyfriend
a happy family
the best year of my life
seventeen, and i'm stealing his belt with the
clicker, fastener, of a
chevrolet seatbelt
his blazer
his pliers
his hammer
his belt
when he left
and here i am
the girl who stole orion's belt, a chevrolet seatbelt
no map of the road ahead
unable to use the stars as a guide
because they disappeared

as i sit on the rocks on the river
i smell the water as it splashes
my feet hurt, my lips quiver
and i let myself calm

as i sit in the brush by the river
my feet crumpling dead leaves
breeze kissing, arms shiver
and i peek through

as i sit in a house by the river
i hear fire crackling the wood
hot air, waves deliver
and i do not float

as i sit in a boat on the river
my knees are wet
feet in puddles, moon a sliver
and i am at peace.

one word, for scream and my father

"describe, in one word,
how you feel today"

sick.

i say sick because of the double meaning,
you see
one word, many meanings

i say sick because i spent my night upchucking
everything i could upchuck and blowing it out of my
nostrils while the stomach acid burned my nose hairs
away

i say sick because i lie in bed feverish and bare-
skinned bodied and sprawled with a book nestled under
my chin like a violin

i say sick because i am also tired, fatigued, and
tired of
        saying what i said

i am sick of not being able to recall honest
apologies and then receiving "i'm sorries" from him

i am sick of seeing him in my head and then without
warning seeing him in those brown skinny jeans

he's a young han solo

"i love you" "i know"

and my father and my attacker
        i am sick of them

i am sick of being sick to my stomach because i am
sick of you

how can i describe in one word the sickness i have
felt for too many years

i am sick of the eye pain after even two tears

i am sick of rhyming and being a perfect writer

i'll never be a perfect writer

and even if i were it wouldn't be seen as labor to
you

haven't you put me through enough labor

i am sick
        and sick
        and tired
        and tired

my name is only one letter away from anger
what else do you expect me to be?
dropping small sacrifices at your feet
singing for you to preach for me
vouch for you
you didn't mean any harm by harming me
maybe you should have named me monica
as in harm-monica
so you could play me
in your prison cell
without guilt again
or just lie to me
like the books you read
that told you mom and i were crazy
for someone so interested in freud you
void intrusive questioning
didn't you know he said that was the best and only
way to learn?
you have not learned anything
and until you do
do not talk to me
do not contact me
saying my voicemail box is full
it's full of you
and your tears, and your threatening
angry angel sings to you
"you are no god,
no heavenly father"

if i wanted you to haunt me the way you do
i would've asked you to
but why would i ask you to

your smile leaves a bad taste in my mouth
sickeningly sweet
like a cupcake
or a raspberry
kiss

i see myself shattering the glass on the floor
and it reads "ungrateful"

or do you know he is perfect?
did you know you would break me
like shattered glass
am i ungrateful?

five mutual
he still sees you
and your body
and your words

his family still sees you

am i just another girl

do you plan on coming back again
i fear you coming back again
the embodiment of everything i've never been

if i wanted you to come for him
i would've asked you to
but why would i ask you to
does he ever ask you to
does he ever ask for you
too

by all things, my grace and dignity have been
stripped from me

dear diary

let me be as beautiful
as gorgeous
as the ones suggested to me

for your safety
i would not suggest coming near me
i would not suggest stepping near me
holding the baby
smiling your smile
your cheekbones protruding
for your safety
i would not suggest letting me see your cheekbones
i would not suggest letting me see any part of you
i will have the urge to break
or snap, or fracture
don't let me smell you
for your safety
keep all of your blood inside of you
i'm a shark, doll
and i'm not afraid to sink my teeth into you

withdrawals (codependent or aching?)

my hands fidget and my arm shakes
it feels like feathers are dancing
upon my spine
and chills
or an itch
i can't tell

breathing is hard with so much gum
and words
stuck in your throat
in your mouth
my tongue hurts
make my tongue hurt

i hold my knuckles in my other hand
and the urge to break them
in my wrist
i feel like a drug addict
is it?
then i am.

distraction.

failed.

itchy sides, and neck, and mind
i can't scratch that
can i
i hope not to harm
place blame
metaphors...

you.
the only feeling on my body until now
has been
longing for you
to hold me
my backache

i chew gum to replace the urges
and the pain in my kneecaps
the black holes in my tonsils
the ulcer
i feel the perforated lines from my teeth
with my tastebuds

shake.

me.

fleas crawl under my skin
but they don't bite me
or are they leeches
pulsating?
either way, they want my blood.

i see a girl scratching her arm
and what i would kill to be in her place
pressing my wrist on the edge of the computer i type
on
blatant
my molars shoot like cavity-ridden comets
seal them in

hold me in
hold me
i need you
or do i?
codependent
or aching?

be gentle with me, especially days like today

i take a second
to walk to the bathroom
as i look my reflection in the eyes
and make my decision

i sigh
and begin rummaging around for metal or sharp plastic
maybe even an applicator i can snap
but all i can find is a bag of small teeth flossers

i put my fingers in between the space in it
and try to pull it apart
but i'm not strong enough
so i run the end along my fingertip, a test

i pull it back in my right hand like an arrow
springing back and forth, stabbing
into my arm, the target
i am a limber bow

the scar from november is my bullseye
and i keep hitting it
scratching at the surface, back and forth
intersecting with ghosts of cutter's past

to leave little red bubbles
and polka dots
and stars, constellations
i hurt myself

                    a poem written whilst staring, in awe, of
                                    the one i truly love

        the weight on my fingers is incredibly strong
        and i'm sorry if i bore you
        because i am sleep deprived
        and exhausted
        but also thoroughly confused as to why you put up
        with me
        and say that you love me
        and run your hands through my hair as if it were
        strands of swarovski crystals and million dollar
        pearls
        your eyes glisten like they were beaten by rain but
        now face the sunlight
        and your smile is a vile of poisonous gin that makes
        me instantly hallucinate the movement of muscles in
        my face
        your teeth like petals of beautiful daisies
        or are they calla lilies
        i want to feel them upon me
        how do you look at me the way you do
        like a statue of juliet
        heartbreakingly, hauntingly
        i don't want you to fall away from me
        can you stand or do you need my help
        all i want to do is help you
        if it means you will stay
        although i may never understand why you would
        no one else did so.

how can your weakness be the same as the source of
your strength
day after day
leaving my knees knocked and my breath stricken from
me
i lie in bed awaiting you walking in and i long for
your touch
your body
the heat radiating from your bare chest to my cheeks
am i blushing or is it just the blood rising
signifying my longing for you
how i am longing for you
you walk into the room and lie down with me
the feeling of your hand wiping the tears from my
cheek
your body heat
calming me yet still sending me into a frenzy
i miss you.
my weakness.
my strength.
my muse.
the air of my breath, the human body, the heat
my spine.
you are the one thing i long for, your touch, your
hands
your life
and your liveliness
breathing life into me
as we drift to sleep.

i felt safe when you touched me

i remember the first time you held me
i had never felt anything like it before
to know, yet still not knowing
not realizing
i felt safe when you touched me.
i remember seeing you under the streetlights
then you held me to your chest
and when you pushed me away
i just wanted to go back
i felt safe when you touched me.
i remember every time i was away from you
i'd imagine your arms around me
and i was upset with myself
it's been a year and i still feel you
but i can finally say,
i can finally realize
i feel safe when you touch me.

i can't wait to be with you everyday
and just be
to wake in a fearful sweat
and see your face in front of me
to come home everyday, stressed
and lay my head on your chest
to let you take me to places i've never been before
to let your presence make me
finally
happy
truly
happy
completely
happy
happily
complete

poetry weather: april 16th, 2018

as i look down on the river from the coffee shop
windows
high tide and brown from the tornado
i think of you
and how your hair fell and blew
while the water misted my face
and your laugh

how our love is like crashing rapids upon rocks
and confessional phone calls
tops of the trees and poems about beauty
the not-so-finer, yet beautiful things
the diamonds in the rough
and peddleboats in a thunderstorm

you sweep me off of my feet
like the leaves
caught in the rain
when i can't swim, you are my life jacket
my wheelbarrow, my beer barrel raft
afloat in the pacific

you're the rocks i can stand on
when i need a bit of support
not the most stable
but that's just how i like it
the concrete bridge covered in hydrogen peroxide
that we stay behind to kiss upon

my cherry blossom petal pulley puller
my serotonin lever keeper
love letter receiver
the hub, the home of all of everything i could ever
want
let me reassure you
i love you
and long for your touch

lollipop sticks

am i your drug of choice
        my love

or do you prefer the cocaine
        you ate off of her fingers

like they were lollipop sticks

satan is my boyfriend

all i want is my love to be laying with me
unholy matrimony
you to be with me
my beautiful sinner
two beautiful sinners
hold me in your poison ivy arms
(i only wish you could love me as i love you)
i only wish i could make you feel something

                    a "too bad" dinner mint poem, and a
                                          toothpick

you don't know how hard it is to speak to you
how many tears i've shed in midnight cars,
boyfriends' laps
mourning the death of my father
the facade he presented to me my whole life
fading

sitting across from you in my favourite pizzeria
wondering how you can look the same
sound the same
but be so different from the father i knew
your reflection taking form in an italian mural
mt. vesuvius slowly erupting

don't forget you are the one who blamed me
any chance he got
a girl should know her place, under her father's
wing, slowly beating by
loudly squawking
"get off your ass"
"i'm recovering"

"i'm in remission"
i don't know how to feel
i can worry less that you're slowly dying
without me, while i'm still mad at you
for always being mad at me
sadly, i don't get to see
whether or not my hypothesis was correct
that the endless pills made you target your own
daughter

be careful
sicily sees
what you say to us
and me
grabbing his hand a little tighter

under the table
instead of crying

romanis running
caravan
carry me
away

NORFOLK AND WESTERN
518654

NORFOLK & WESTERN
CABOOSE #518654

This Norfolk & Western caboose was given to the
City of Burlington by Norfolk Southern Railway in 1993. It
is symbolic of the railroad roots of the North Carolina
Railroad town of Company Shops (1865) which became
Burlington in 1893. The caboose was painstakingly
restored in 2006-2007 and is now a museum depicting
life aboard a train as it was when a caboose rolled behind
every freight.

Available for guided tours by appointment.
Call the Burlington Recreation & Parks Department
Monday-Friday 336.222.5030

cannibal hallucinations and cannabis
hallucinogens

a hypothetical
i get rid of lipstick stains with a pencil eraser
and the friction burns me
creates a hole
and the shavings light a little when they hit bone

she draws pictures for me
pictures of sex, and me, love, bonnets, and poisonous
things
questions and experiments and children's faces
to linger and spook you
flashlights

mix a vanilla coke and fireball in a ball jar
a bell jar
and tell sylvia i haven't written about her
suicide for this book yet
and i'm not planning to
unless she asks me herself

my baby protects me
growling at him
as he bites at my feet
through the white fleece
reading "angel"
and the flowery sheets

and she reaches for my teardrops like feathers
falling from the skies of my mind

and moths, grasshoppers

addison, get them
addison, save me

once again

                the modern love affair: waiting for, and
                            dreadfully missing, my love

a modern love affair includes
pleading with your mother to let you stay with your
lover for the weekend
after all, you're an adult
and you'll go anyhow.

he sleeps hours away
and i look at the stars knowing he looks at them too
but the glimmer in the skies will
never compare to the one in his eyes
when he looks at me
i feel beautiful
i feel whole.

i wonder when he'll respond.

a modern love affair is looking at a folder of
photographs titled his name and a black heart
and thinking he may be looking at one of you
but that he's probably working to get to a point
where we can be together
and stay together
and never have to say goodbye for weeks again.

"the victim to abuser cycle," my screen
reads, giving my fear an address

"will I become more abusive? what if I already have?"
reads the name of the article
the question
questions
after i asked mine
"are abuse victims more likely to become abusers"
i type
i pray
i will not become him
my love
will not become them
darling, what if we become them
if we dispose of them, their images
will they fade
or will they live on
inside
of us?

body

a part of me is still in love with him
scream
your first love never leaves your mind, nor your
heart
and in my dreams he offered me cinnamon cigarettes
and alcohol
afterall,
he is dangerous
and left a lasting scar on my mind, my heart
my memories, and my body:
        attacked, raped, and taken from me.

little skeleton boy with a broken, bumpèd nose
and i love that he can't smell the stench
of vomit on my clothes from crying too hard
and his colorblind eyes
can't see the blood from the glass shards

i bust my head into/in two

"i don't know why i love you, but i do" he said,
as we laid on our bed
"if i did, it wouldn't be love, would it?"
he asked, as a tear fell down onto my cheek
to my breast
as if i knew

what he said
was so beautiful
but so terrifying

but what has he ever said
or done
that wasn't
so beautiful
but so terrifying

and that's why i love him
or is it?

i like ripped pages and
discolored marks and scars

gel pens overflowing and the
etymology of everything

i like to be curious but
find it is reckless of me

dangerous for me, but wild
and spontaneous

i like my leather jacket
despite its tears and flakes

and the many times my mother
tells me i'm not allowed to wear it

i like rebellion in the sense
something good will come out of it

and picketing, and protesting,
chaos for the good of the people

i like braids on black
women and natural dark skin

stretch marks and smile lines
and oxfordian accents

i like bags that are too small
and late night rambling

laughing and shrieking but
only hearing noise complaints

i like metal concerts and
catching bible pages

crying and screaming and
old ladies holding permanent markers

i like poise and originality
in the sense of personality

you and your happiness
for making me happy

i like clothes and expression
but appreciate the bare body

the curvature and the variation
the culture and the differentiation

i like life and the people and
the strangers and the family

and the friendship, and the hardship,
and the chaos, and the love

i like life despite the times
i wish it were taken from me

i love life and the people
that made it lovely for me

but he left me
but he didn't need me
but i've never known him
but he has become my villain
he looked down on me

but he never did
"but not anymore"

changed
hurt me
left me
love me

goodbye

about me

hi. my name is angel elizabeth matthews, i grew
up in burlington, north carolina and everything
about me and my life is broadcasted to the public
through books. but that's okay. i wouldn't prefer
it anyway else.

i'm finding a way
        to learn
what love is
and maybe it is because of you, father
        who taught me i was wrong
or maybe it was you, scream
        who taught me what was wrong
no
i think it was you, austin
        who taught me how to feel instead
        of think. and not to hope too
        hard. to enjoy the moment.
the little things. the experience
        who taught me it didn't matter
        what happened to me. it mattered
        that i was happy.
and that above all, i mattered
        despite how the other men who
        i thought taught me made
                me feel
you made me feel love.
        in its truest form
and for that, i thank you
                i love you.

and the people

the people who looked out for me,
        cared for me, aunt teri. all of you
all of you helped me redefine the idea
        of love.

finally: what is love?
it is the songs you danced to when you were seven
years old
the people who texted you "you matter"
the people who looked you in the

        eyes and said "you belong here"
addi's purr, houdini's meow, miley's oily fur
the feeling of breathing and knowing
                you made it this far
laughing with your friends, making out in a car
feeling safe in those situations you thought you'd
never feel safe in
                again

my mother's smile
my brother's unenthusiastic side-hugs

and a blonde, six foot tall
        blue eyed doll called austin.

you all taught me.
you helped me find my way.

you let me finally fall in love.

                you are love
                        to me.

photos courtesy of lizz matthews, beth matthews,
and daniel slagell.